AND I ALONE ESCAPED TO TELL YOU

D1596099

And I alone escaped to tell you

SYLVIA D. HAMILTON

GASPEREAU PRESS LIMITED
PRINTERS & PUBLISHERS
MMXIV

1

Then deep from the earth you shall speak, from low in the
dust your words shall come; your voice shall come from
the ground like the voice of a ghost, and your speech shall
whisper out of the dust.

ISAIAH 29:4

And the Sabeans fell upon them, and took them away; yea,
they have slain the servants with the edge of the sword
and I only am escaped alone to tell thee.

JOB 1:15

THE PASSAGE

AFTER ROBERT HAYDEN
*Voyage through death
to life upon these shores.*

We had our own names
a past a present.
We worked we loved.
Sang songs to the wind
prayed to our Gods.

We did not know the future
would not be ours.

We fought. And we fought.

And when we were spent
terrors, like a buzz of locusts
invaded our sleep, night terrors,
not chased away by the morning sun,
night terrors stalking us.

And when we went crazy with pain
sinking into the dank water, blood
rushing from the hole in our chests

still the terrors danced on our bodies,
waiting, waiting to overtake the next ones—
shackled below on the *Severn* in full sail
behind us.

The sons of darkness stole our children's tomorrow.

... slaves by habit and education
LORD DALHOUSIE

1.

My name is Byna. This is my cousin Sylla. Joseph Wilson owns our bodies.
He has a farm in Windsor. We pick vegetables in his fields, we pull apples
from his trees. In his house, we cook, we clean, make his bed. We tend his
children. Heal him when he fall sick. Sylla can't remember the year—
I can, 1776—when he wrote his death paper. We never be free.
When he sleep, we go to his private room, quiet quiet pull open his drawer,
find the paper. When he die, we pass to son Jonathan—forever and ever
and ever. I want to tear it to shreds, set it alight until I see his name—
the witness, a proper judge of this Nova Scotia.

Cousin Sylla's hand stop me. She save my life.

2.

Sylla's walk that night was uneventful,
at 4 AM she wanted it that way.

The stillness crept up behind her,
she thought maybe she should have brought Cato
for a last time before Wilson sell him off too.

At ten years, he would still walk any time.
Perhaps his internal clock was timeless,
not remembering morning or night.

She was glad the damn heat bugs were gone.
Crickets to others—heat bugs to her clan.
When young that's what
Uncle called them:

those damn heat bugs
make so much noise
person can't sleep.

So here it was she walked the path to the barn,
guided by the late leaving moon.
Inside to sit, waiting for the sun,
for her calm to return,
for her body to give itself over
once again to the day.

DINAH'S LETTER TO HER SISTER

Shelburne, 10 November 1784

Daphne

I write to you though I know your tired hands may never touch this paper. We been here ten year now. An agreeable place sometimes. A boychild came last year after much labour. Makes us five. Granny Hannah thought the ancestors might take him and he would not look into my face, the caul was thick thick. Instead Amos mother joined them in her 85th year. By sea one day we will journey far and Amos take Samuel's caul from its secret place to protect us. Sleep visits not often after the lash. They all spoke ill of me in court. You remember Thomas Robertson and that Mrs. Hayes.

The two stood together against me. Their friends in the jury box would not hear my words, guilty they said. Saturday last a day of first snow my body counted to one hundred before my spirit lifted me up and the jailer lashed one hundred more. Joshua, my first born, overtook the jailer from behind before they jump him force him to the ground. He just a boy but they make him lie in that wet cold jail. Rats wait in every corner. He throw the rotten food in their face. I pray God he will not suffer the lash. I hear him singing quiet quiet. As sun rises, my body will swallow fifty more. This time Amos promise to hide my babies in the church house. Granny Hannah give me her special ribbon for my mouth. Now the night releases itself I must go prepare.

Dear sweet sweet Daphne, I long to see your face again.

Always with love
Your sister Dinah

TRACADIE

1.

The warm summer breeze arrived at the 7th hour.
See the young emerald green pheasant
strutting across the path in front of my door.
Above me pastel blue, almost white sky,
puffy clouds, the kind Jesus will surely step out from.

Dying on the longest day of the year.

A longer death or longer
to remember my death.

2.

This land does not forgive. We cut our way
in tangled forests. Backs ache, hands, feet bruised
bodies broken. Ma name me Manuel. He call me John.
Write my name on his death paper with his bed,
pinchbeck watch, gold seal, silver spectacles—one glass missing.
He pass on my body to his son, not my spirit.
It already asleep with the ancestors.

On Saturday next, at twelve o'clock, will be sold on the Halifax Beach, two hogshead of rum, three of sugar and two well-grown Negro girls, aged fourteen and twelve, to the highest bidder.

1.

Thursday waited for the tides to leave.
She walked the sand out to the island
taking her footprints with her. She was not hiding.
Just not where that indenture paper say she should be.
The gulls, her watchers. The blueberries and sea kelp
her food. The evergreen boughs, her bed.

2.

She descend over rocks flat and jagged.
Some say she fly with the gulls. Some say
that whale wait for her just off shore.
Some say she that odd rock stuck—look *there*
last spit of land before the sea open.
Some say she that wave smash high, high
hugging hard rock face trying not to return to sea.

tout wench stout fellow fine girl healthy s
rom Madagascar stout healthy negro sto
ye fine boy stout healthy negress stout m
tout lad thin wench stout healthy man lik
orn out born free stout child stout mulat
irl low wench stout mulatto likely boy squ
n each cheek lame of left arm small boy s
stout small wench stout and tall stout sh
ade black wench stout brickmaker rema
ach cheek thin weakly wench thin pilot b
rdinary man pilot by orders thin looking
ellow stout black wench squat scar over r
tout sizeable wench mulatto stout fellow
ttle wench slow well sized man tall limbe
ade fellow ordinary wench almost past
emarkable fine wench stout black stout s
orn out ordinary fellow sound sizeable m

ench worn out healthy young woman mu
ro boy healthy negress healthy blind in ri
ut boy ordinary wench stout sayer & labo
d healthy mulatto wench born free nearly
f indian stout blind of an eye thick mulat
nch stout black low lad stout wench 3 sca
ench thick lips pockmarked remarkably
nch stout scar on the point of left eye slin
y stout & lusty scars on right arm 3 long s
r thin wench mulatto stout fellow stout w
small wench stout yellow wench squat st
e 3 marks between eyes sick wench tall ar
o fine wench stout black fellow a cooper s
h stout fine fellow old & worn wench stou
ur lusty squat wench very short ordinary
uilt wench slender fellow sickly man tall
e boy stout wench stout fellow fine girl he

SHELBURNE

> *I give and bequeath to my loving wife Sarah Herbert, my*
> *Negro woman Venus and to my son Thomas, my slave Isaac.*
> WILL OF JOHN HERBERT, 1 MARCH 1799

At the well a thin layer of ice cracks when poked with a stick
or the rim of her bucket. On colder days a small hatchet
carves a hole wide enough for the bucket to sink through.
Hold tight to the rope he says. Slow, slow, slow.
Laughter echoes up like water brimming over the bucket's edge.
Replace the wooden cover. Careful of splinters, Isaac says.

In sweet July Kellum's Brook reflects faces looking in.
Venus, skirt pulled high above her glistening knees straddles
the rushing flow at the deepest point. Glancing at Isaac
she dips her bucket into the rushing foam.

Face lowered, eyes closed mouth wide against the quickening stream.
Soft spray caresses smooth faceskin. Lips catch, drink.
A fleeting kiss of lovers' last embrace.

LOYALIST VOYAGE

1.

Clear crisp day sun deceives,
feel the fingers of cold air on my cheek
moving up my face to my eyes.

2.

Winter wind catches our sails
pushing us through the harbour.
I must look, look into this
dark water that surrounds us.

3.

Trees on the coast
almost gone now from view.
Bits of ice crust my shawl.

4.

On the *Lucretia* night smells foul below.
I come above, sit to breathe the cool air.
Mother give me life one hundred four year ago.
I say my story to myself every night before sleep.
When day come, I tell all who will listen.

Yes, John Clarkson say, there will be trees
in Sierra Leone, shall I ever see them.
Will we ever see this place
this Freetown?

APOLLOS

Ran away on 12 March 1810,
Apollo 1 & Apollo 2, aged 23 and 24 ...

Water slices through the cracks of rocks
forming pools, traces of snow and sand.

1.

Iron-clad wrists cuffed together,
bare feet bruised bloody.
Cudjoe and Congo sank into
the dense forest.

Brothers
by blood and love
by soot and smoke
by iron and coal.

Leaving behind his names
and a souvenir of their trade:
a smith's nail hammered his right palm
to the bedpost where their Ma died.
Where he prayed but death would not answer.

2.

Cudjoe took his fine leather bellows,
Congo, his prized brass hammer.
Praying an oath on her grave, they vowed
never to part. They fashioned
one small key to fit the cuffs.
Each in turn keeping it safe.

BY SOME OTHER NAME

breath

wait until night fall   creep
into the forest bowels
run
     crawl
             roll
down

jagged

hills   *breath*

wade

deep   inkblack   lake

bog   sucking   swollen feet

away   slip   *breath*

bloody fingers   claw moss

breath

gasping   grasping

hand upon hand   *breath*

before come the moon

MELVILLE ISLAND

1814

Silenced by the snow
they wondered if even God
had finally forsaken them

home a stone prison
temporary officials say
we used to temporary

come in from the fields one day
to find out we been up and sold
we invented temporary

when they line us up
after they drag us
off them waterbeds of death
we ready for a new kind of temporary

nova scarcity
seed potatoes turnip tobacco
good crop in the fall
now all froze to the floor

and if we still here
in spring
we try again

LOVETT LAKE

Easter 1816

He moves through
our River Jordan
gently breaking
the skin of ice
thick as his black robe.

Prayers running hot
through his heart,
a shield against
the deepening chill.

Words dance along
his cold breath
making their way
to singing converts,
each waiting their turn.

He signals,

The Great Baptizing begins.

MARTHA

Liverpool, 1822

1.

She walks the town, tired of digging.
She's gone you know, they all say,
gone. It's the fever. Careful,
speak to her kindly, be gentle of voice.
She won't know you. Say her dress is pretty,
ask how she sew on so many buttons. Smile,
she'll do same in return. Take your leave.

2.

Martha digs holes round her hut
trying to get back there. If she
digs deep enough, she'll find them—
all three there waiting.
Miriam will care for Rose and Aaron,
Martha taught her well.

3.

Joshua's gone too. It's the fever. Martha keeps
the tattered twice-folded paper tucked in her apron:

He will no doubt endeavour to pass for a free man possibly by some other name.
Known to his owner J. Hicks as Bill Hicks. Reward offered.

She hopes he'll never come home.

AMBROSE SMART

Cape Negro, Purgatory Point, 15 January 1827

1.

He did not know I mean to kill him. Hannah know.
She took my knife from its secret pocket in my boot.

I fix my left hand round his throat,
I reach for my blade —it gone.
His sons jump me from behind, knock me down.
He cough and sware, sware and cough: he say
Hannah is my property you hear mine.
I spit in his red pockmark face.

Hang me now or sell me. None of you safe
long as God give me breath.

2.

Hannah's hands could no longer caress him with desire.
Sometimes Ambrose paid for more nimble ones
showing no signs of age or despair.

3.

At Cape Negro, northeast of Port La Tour,
the voice of the sea was strong that night
raging until dawn, when the fog—smothering her
like the soft wool blanket her granny
spun before her birth—arrived
to choke the sunrise.

Hannah couldn't see the ocean on Sunday
but felt its pull especially on long summer days
after the solstice, before come the full moon.

4.

And I alone escaped to tell you.

JCH LEDGER: JOHN COOPER HAMILTON

Glynn County, Georgia, 25 November 1834

1.

By the candle's somber light,
Daphne watched him writing
in his book again.

2.

Someday one day
Someone will know about us.
On my mother's grave I believe
this true.

Dinah and her children
mortgaged to James Butler
for one hundred dollars and eight cows.
Now ten months later, we have them back.

His feather marks their age and the day
of their return.

And of my cousins who stole
freedom ten marks ago,†
no word I only believe they safe.

I hear he having troubles,
he may lose this place.
If he need money, we first to be sold.

Winter like death
comes too soon.

† *She carved marks into the bark of the oak tree in the far field, one mark for each year.*

Digby, 21 June 1792

Run Away, Joseph Odel and Peter Lawrence, Negroes, from their masters, and left Digby last evening. The first mentioned is about twenty-four years of age five feet six inches high, had on a light brown coat, red waistcoat and thicker Breeches, but took other clothes with him, he is a likely young fellow with remarkable white Teeth. — The other is about five feet eight inches high, very Black, had on lighghteh coloured Clothes — Whoever will secure said Negroes so that their Masters may have them again, shall receive TEN DOLLARS Reward, and all reasonable Charges paid. —DANIEL ODEL, PHILIP EARL

1. HMS DIOMEDE, HALIFAX HARBOUR, 13 SEPTEMBER 1813

I sick again in the morning time no wonder
move my fork to pick the food it move too
how they think we eat this maggoty gruel
pick out what I can eat the rest
it don't stay down long

Ambrose Smart say we about two thousand now
all come here with little but our name never mind
we don't know our name the one
we had before they stole us long before I born

Hear talk pretend I can't they don't want us here
one of them say governor going to stop ships from coming
We British subjects now pains them We the same as they

2. CHARLES MORRIS

Charles Morris laying out some land for us they say nearby

3. LITTLE SARAH, REFUGEE HILL, 20 FEBRUARY 1815

That winter a storm of measles passed through leaving Little Sarah and her cousins blind, sick, or dead. Snatched and dragged along the ground, the ragged piece of cotton she tore from her mother's dress held tight in her tiny hand.

Caleb Jones refused to take Sarah as part of his purchase. What good is Flora if she has to carry this blind child everywhere. After Philip Earl sold off her mother and her baby brother Lidge to Jones, Sarah lived with Uncle Pompey.

At fifteen she was no longer little but she was still blind.

4. BLACK WOMAN ANN, OTHERWISE CALLED NANCY

*Flora, weak from the pox. Ben carried her on his back until he couldn't
walk himself. Solomon waited to cover our steps. We parted at the
southeast bend of the river where the white spruce grew tall and thick.*

Holding the paper close to her eyes Ann cracks the small window ajar
enough for slivers of sunlight to pass through. Lidge sits beside her, one
hand bothering the beetle he found in the corner, in the other, the little
boat Ben carved for him.

*There. Page 7. Caleb Jones announcement. The Saint John Royal Gazette.
He may find some of us but not soon. Six dollars for me,
Flora and Lidge. Two guineas each for Solomon and Ben.*

5. FLORA

Leave me. Go. I'll rest here awhile. What can they do worse
than this damn pox. You promised Lidge you'd find him,
carve him a bigger boat. Go. Find them. Find Ann.

Flora smudged mud and moss into her white cotton jacket.
Humming

By and by when the morning comes
When all the saints of God are gathering home
We will tell the story how we overcome
And we'll understand it better by and by

Her petticoat ripped into strips to wrap her cracked, bloody feet.

The last of her biscuit and smoked trout
she stuffed into her sack before sleep came.

6. BEN

Ankle broken. Back stiff. Heart heavy. No sign of Solomon.
He was not at the meeting place. He peels the bark from
a length of birch thick as his arm. That'll do. His blade dulled
from cutting boughs and sods needs sharpening. Whittle this
new boat for Lidge. Spruce gum to secure the small masts.
The remnant of Flora's petticoat for the sail.

7. CYRUS, PRESTON, 13 DECEMBER 1816

Cold cold so cold. This year summer never came.
Would that the crusts of snow caked
against the timbers be sugar for my bitter tea.

Yesterday   Cyrus 4th born day   He outside now
calling   calling   calling   for his little brown barker.

Wait   I tell him   Look see   the starlight.

He come back by and by.

No heart to tell him

Sam Biddell and them ate well last night.

25 June 1829

Rose Cooper Free Woman of Colour
Naparina, Trinidad

My Cousin

If you read this, Levin's journey was safe. He will speak our news to your
waiting ears. This season wild apples came less plentiful than last year.
I made dry what I could for you before his ship sailed. There you have
plenty plenty sugar to make them sweet for Naomi and James to eat. I
remember how they love them so. We wait to hear from Mr. C. about our
petition for money to repair the road. Every family gave their name. So
many rocks and ruts, and winter after winter, our carts break. One horse
die. If we can't make market to sell the brooms and charcoal, there's little
to eat, save for what we pull from this ungenerous soil.

More come to me every day with troubles. My wormwood and
elderflowers almost gone now. I no longer welcome the walk to the
barrens for more. Granny Ruth says surely it will be a boy, my third born.
She's getting on but now Liza helps her bring the babies, so many already
this year. But Cousin you are not here. Day by day I dread they will lock
irons on you again like Peggy. Her Free Paper they burned. Levin tells me
many there are chained. The lies. Enough sadness. Remember how you
always watched for the chickadees? They still call and play hide and seek
for you at dusk, fluttering the full leaves on the maples, waiting for your
return.

May God stand beside you
Your loving cousin Cloey

THREE PHEASANTS

came before the snow
before the flight of a
thousand gulls, before
the wind awoke, before
the baby who arrived still
before she stood at
the door of hope.

2

*My skin is black upon me, and my
bones are burned with heat.*

JOB 30:30

EXCAVATION

1.

I am not the navigator on this journey.
I am more than a passenger, but not the captain.
Longing for that which is not,
for what could have been,
for that imagined place.

2.

I found my life as I once knew it:
c. 1964 an honest coloured girl.

Look at me.
I watched Howdy Doody, Mickey Mouse,
Razzle Dazzle, Maggie Muggins, Gunsmoke,
Bonanza, Ed Sullivan, Frank's Bandstand,
Don Messer and His Islanders, Singalong Jubilee,
Gazette, Front Page Challenge, Hockey Night in Canada.

I had my secret decoder ring
and my mini plastic submarine—
I filled it with baking soda so it would
move underwater in the enamel basin.

3.

Toronto, 1966.
Le Coq D'Or Tavern.
Singapore slings and patent leather pumps:
I'm 16, they'll think I'm 21.

4.

My sisters love to jive. I used to watch them through
the small window at Art's Canteen. We'd take
turns, boosting each other up to peek in. Who they dancing
with now, I'd ask my cousins when it was my turn
to hold the feet of the next peeker. We were too young
to get in and had already been kicked out more than once.

Now they jive together any chance they get:
a wedding usually. And they still own the floor.

5.

My brother was a bricklayer,
then he joined the army
went to Egypt
saw the Great Pyramids
and wondered
what his life would have been
like if he'd been born there
instead of here.

He lived in Germany and
went to Holland.
When he came home
he used to bring us
pomegranates, a special treat.
Taught me how to
gently suck the red seeds
to extract the bitter sweet juice.

He used to make the best French fries.
We'd pretend he was the cook:
Sell them to us for five cents in
his homemade chip cup—
wax paper (from the eaten bread loaf)
twisted into shape.
Don't tell Mom
he charged us.

I'd laugh, he'd make me dance,
show off what his baby sister could do.
The back breaker:
on bended knees
lean, lean, lean back

until my back was flat to the floor,
to Fats Domino, Jerry Butler—
his favourites.
Now he's gone
and would not talk about his leaving.

6.

When I finally
got her attention—
Size 7 and a half please
as I reached for the shoe—

contempt, veiled
as laughter:
You can't afford those!

At that moment
I resolved to try on
every Size 7 and a half
in the store.

Not that I would ever buy
only that I would try.

She needed to know
I had the right,
if I chose to,
try and buy whatever
she had to show.

Very politely, *the grey pumps, please.*
The *Amalfi in green.*
(I hate green)
Canvas Deck, why not.

When she was finally
surrounded by boxes,
her face truly red
I left shoeless.
Only Imelda would not be pleased.

7.

SCHOOL DAYS

English Level 4, Book 2 ©1962

Lesson: *Listen to the Language*

I worked like a _____.

He's a real _____ driver.

She _____ over a hot stove
all day to cook his supper.

He cracked the _____ to make
them work harder.

Today's Announcements

INT. HIGH SCHOOL— DAY. C. MAY 1966

FADE UP: EMPTY PALE HOSPITAL-GREEN HALLWAY, BEIGE
LOCKERS ON BOTH SIDES:

IN VOICE-OVER, MALE VOICE, THE PRINCIPAL

*... And next week will be our slave auction. All those participating must
remember that you can't have your slave do anything that is illegal or
embarrassing. Only those students participating will be allowed to attend
the school dance on Friday. Funds raised will go to the student council.
The glee club will meet today at noon in the Library. The boys' basketball
team will have a home game ...*

CROSSFADE

8.

COMPUTER BASICS

CUT TO:

INT. COMPUTER LAB—NIGHT. C. SEPTEMBER 1981

DIMLY LIT. OVERHEAD LONG TUBE LIGHTS—ONE BLINKS ON
AND OFF, ON AND OFF. GROUP OF TIRED LOOKING ADULTS,
ABOUT EQUAL WOMEN AND MEN, SITTING AT COMPUTER
STATIONS. PERKY FEMALE INSTRUCTOR IN FRONT:

OK group, ready to begin? This is Computer Basics 100, Introduction
to MS DOS. Power-up your computer. Sorry—computer speak. That
means, turn it on. [*Nervous giggle*] The switch is on the back of that
tall box on your desk beside that thing that looks like a TV. We call it a
monitor.

ANGLE ON—CU MONITOR AS IT POWERS UP—FLICKERING
WORDS APPEAR:

Master   Slave   Master   Slave

1.

The docent doesn't like children
but didn't know it.

She had been a teacher, she said.
That explained it.

This is what you see in the painting.
See the lines. Remember the lines.

They will not remember the lines.
Her tone, they will remember.

2.

Hitler's Jawbone on Display in Russia, 25 April 2000.

The children wondered
what the jawbone of a monster looked like.

Was it gigantic?
Did it smell bad?
What colour was it?

The docent led them
Through the Palaeolithic period.

Soon, we'll see it. Very soon.

What if there were other
jawbones on display?
How will we know
the right one they wondered.

*In this room I want you
to pay attention to the central display case.
You will see fragments of a meteorite found in 1962 ...*

They didn't hear her.

Who will get to look first?
How long can we stay in that room?
Maybe it will be too creepy.

What if the power goes out?

The docent, impatient,
calls to them.

We are going to see
fragments of Hitler's jawbone.
Line up in twos.
Please don't push or shove.

The children stood still.
Maybe we should wait.
Let those adults go first.

3.

At the Little Schoolhouse Museum
I found Bunga and Simba
just where I left them
frozen in *Visits in Other Lands,*
recognized the green textured cover,
large lettering along its spine.

In case I forgot how to say
their names, there's a How To Pronounce Guide
at the back of the book: see page 32.
Bung' a   Sim ba'

Bunga was a Negrito boy,
Simba, a boy from the deep Congo.

They look out at me
with simple inquiring stares,
wondering where I've been
these past forty years.
They don't recognize me at all.
I've changed. And they?

Still trapped, half naked,
between these musty pages
on which childlike words
of explanation seem innocent:

Bunga has his breakfast.
Simba returns to his
home on the Congo—

In a boat carrying
White passengers above deck and
Negroes with dark shiny skin,

Negroes wearing few clothes,
ride below, taking no notice of the
animal life, the abundant
greenery, for this is their home.

I tell them I know.
I know now what
I didn't know then.

I know about Lucy, the Olduvai Gorge,
the Ashanti, the Dogon, the Yoruba,
the Masai, Nefertiti, the Great Pyramids.

I wish I could take them home with me.

The matter of who did or did not have Black blood, while not a frequent subject of discussion in the white section of town, hung around quietly in the wings, like an understudy waiting for that moment to be called forth. Whispered stories only after children were supposed to be asleep in their beds. In the Black neighbourhood, it came up often, and with precision:

"You see how fast that daughter of Rita Delaney up and got married and moved away."

"Yep and her poor cabby-headed fool of a husband don't even know what kind of goods he got. Goes to the dry goods store to get some one hundred percent cotton and comes out with some kind of something else."

"Ain't that the truth. Her folks saw she was getting just a little too close to that boy of Daisy's."

"Rita knew darn well she wasn't going over there to get Wally to help her with her homework. Even came to Church with her brazen self. Sat with them in their family pew and all."

"She take up with Wally you know what them kids'd look. It skipped her, at least Rita thinks so, but *we* can tell."

"That baby pop out with some of that orangey red hair and freckles and there'd be no hiding then."

"No, probably baby be darker."

"Don't matter, no way, it'd show—Rita—she got the *blood* on both sides."

"Both sides? I never knew that. I thought it was just on her mother Irma's side?"

"You remember Hetty Leonard who took up with Doug Jones? Could never marry him of course but he hanged around on the side, yes he did."

"And they tell me on her father's side, way back, one of the brothers was running a coloured woman who moved here from the Boston States. Supposed to be all hush hush."

"It comes out it do. May take some years, but it do. And if you marry pure coloured, it's bound to come out sometime. And they all walk around like they shit don't smell. Think we stupid. Damn! *Mtsssk.*"

Halifax, 1965

Vera hated her name. Was too short. Too simple. Why her parents pick that name? Probably named after someone. Who cares about somebody been dead fifty years. Couldn't they have named her *Samantha*, or *Veronique* even. First thing she do when she get to the city is change her name. Pick a new one. Get some of those little cards printed up. *Miss Veronique Cooper.* With her address. Seen one of those cards only once. Time when that perfect white woman, dressed in that perfect white linen suit came to the house. Left her fancy white card on the dining room table after Mamma asked her—no, told her to leave. Mamma burned it.

Veronique. Sounds different. Sounds French. Sounds important. *Veronique Cooper.* Not Cooper. Something, but not that. Don't work with *Ver-on-nique.* Only thing with this name change was how to make sure she got messages from home. Couldn't very well tell Mamma to ask for Veronique when she called the landlord or—God forbid—Rev. Washington. Would have to make a plan. Tell them, at home, everyone always called her Vera for a nickname. Wouldn't be hard to understand. Everyone had nicknames. Got so there was one man that nobody knew his right name. When he die, write-up in the paper just used his nickname. That was it. Even his last name wasn't his right name. Took the last name of the people what brung him up. Weren't his real folks. Course no one could ask them they all dead now too. So they bury him as Pokey Parsons. A nickname and someone else's last name. Maybe keep her own last name. Least at the Brick House.

Take Cass. He was one of those coffee coloured pretty men. He look like someone Vera seen before in the coloured magazines and newspapers her aunt sent from the Boston States. He savoured her reaction. Was used to it. Enjoyed it. Played her with his eyes. Cass was a musician. Always said music was his calling. And sing. Better than Wilson Pickett. Didn't need no backups. Would do anything for music, except sometimes play music.

56

Perfect. That's how everything had to be for him to perform. Could play almost any instrument. Piano, his favourite. Though after this last move, Lucinda say he couldn't move that piano into their one cramped-up room. Ready for a fight, but decided maybe she was right. Move it to his brother's house. But those damn kids. No doubt they'll mess it up. Teach them a few songs, Lucinda say, they'll respect the piano. Won't damage it. Worth a try. Go there to play piano. Play sax at home. When he feel like he need his space, Cass just take his sax and run.

Coloured girl wanted, live in or out. Cleaning and light housekeeping. Three children. References required. Only serious applicants need apply. Weekly pay: fifty dollars.

Spend a dollar on nylons. Find the black polish for my sister's shoes. Pleated, navy wool skirt and white blouse. Dark and light. For Monday morning. After Sunday evening service, wash the blouse. Will it dry in time? Get up early to get the stove going, heat the flat iron. Watch for scorching. Mamma say always use a pressing cloth.

Waved to the back door, she motions to a chair in the kitchen. A small, brown-haired head peeks around the doorway. *Sit here. How old are you? Have you worked before? Are your parents at home? Both? Do you have reliable transportation? Are you trustworthy? Do you go to church regularly? We expect the highest standards in personal hygiene ...*

Keep my hands folded. Quivering fingers holding tight to each other. Feet together, flat. Stop my right knee from bouncing. *Will* the sweat back. Answer. Speak. Push the words out. The air is still. Words frozen into shards of ice cut my mouth. Spit-blood trickles. Never mind. Swallow. Swallow hard. Speak.

Is there something wrong? Do you have a hearing problem Miss? I don't have all morning. Others are coming. If you're not interested, don't waste my time. You people have to learn sooner or later that you can't waste our time.

She opens the kitchen door. The sound of its closing is final.

3

The poet is not a rolling stone.
He has two sacred obligations: to leave and to return.
PABLO NERUDA

WONDER

Grandmother was bewildered.

She squinted. They looked like her.
Same warm brown skin, coiled
once-black hair, serious smiling eyes.

She didn't understand them.

French, Spanish, German:
words touching, teasing,
dancing past her ears.

They looked like her.
She wondered, were they her people?

Coming close she whispered:
But what language do they laugh in?

CRAZY BLACK LUCE

Here she comes
jingling jangling
slapping her
worn-out tambourine.
Crazy Luce.

Coloured ribbons
floating from her hair.
Round rainbow rounds
growing from her dress.
High button, once shiny shoes.

Sundays were her days special days.
Church service through,
Luce making music
along the dirt road.
Kicking up dust,
making kids laugh tears.

Others say she's crazy,
keep away from her.
Look at her dress:
covered with shiny
rainbow rounds.
Coloured ribbons
floating from her hair.
High boots and full skirts,
never without her tambourine.

Crazy Luce
sang when no one else would sing.
Made music
when there was no music to be made.

Made kids laugh tears
when they thought
they couldn't.

Crazy
Black
Luce.

He was a constellation of memories. Now his two hats sit tucked
away in her closet. She wears one—A Biltmore size seven and
three-quarters, green-grey wool, red-brown side feather.

She thought she knew his stories. The ones he told. The ones held close.
Kept secret. Could she see into that corner where he stored them?
Where he would pull them out, tidy the worn edges, add a thread or two,

and bind them with a sailor's knot. In his quiet she saw the cold path
he carved close behind him when he left.

He is alive in the stillness.

PARADE

A punch of wood smoke, a warm breath of air.
Remember how we used to play majorettes
with a stick snapped from a tree.

Baby jackknife in hand, debark it, scrape away the
knots, but not too smooth. You still need a good grip.
Weight—has to be just right. Too skinny, stick will fall,
not twirl, won't stay up in the air. Too heavy, will crack
your head on its way down.

No pretty spotless white boots with blue tassels. No perfect
accordion style short skirt with matching tailored navy
jacket. No top hat with stars & sparkles. Only tight braids
bound with small ribbons. Only flat hand-me-down white
sneakers, with ankle socks. Knees and legs, dry and ashy
from the wild sun. Cotton madras shorts, a short-sleeve
blouse, a rip or two mended again for the umpteenth time.

Singing on the back porch, under the night sky,
trees our audience, stars our light show.
We were The Shirelles, The Miracles,
The Supremes, the Motown Black backups.

Every sweet lyric pressed to heart,
Every flawless butterfly hand move mimed.
Slow foot sweep, back to front, slide to the side,
a laughing head toss back.

And Patti's high notes stayed just out of reach.
Never mind. In the sweat of summer,
in the soft glow of the rising blue moon, we sang
and swayed and sang some more.

No one told us we couldn't.

1. CANADA DAY, 2003

By an accident of birth I walk the dyke road. Wind sweeps tufts of marsh grass. Purple wild flowers and a tiny black and white bird guide my path. I could be the Ugandan girlchild dropping my books on the floor, fleeing with my cousins throughout the night to safety in the nearest town. Sleeping for an hour before dawn and the trek back home for school. Then, the same again. Hoping against hope to elude the boy rebel kidnappers fuelled by drugs, bent on rape and death.

2. AFTER JUAN

At Lockeport, the sea, upset,
puked piles of gulfweed—
arranged as elegant birds.

At my feet, a mass of sea wrack
like a forgotten animal, defeated
in a desperate attempt to survive
more powerful predators.

The sea could not sing.

3. TURTLE BAY, TOBAGO

Whitecaps and sharp slap of waves. Gulls and pelicans feast at the sea's buffet. A small plume of grey smoke rising on the shore. Watching, waiting for the leatherbacks. Fish, prey to men and birds. The ripple of taut brown shoulder blades, outstretched arms bearing an offering of bamboo. The boat, motor cut, stern tilt, a steady glide out to sea.

4. KITSILANO, VANCOUVER

In this neighbourhood of small dogs, yoga mats and siphon-drippped seven dollar cups of java, I fool myself into thinking all is right with the world. Not another baby dead from malaria, not a girlchild sold as a sex slave, not a sniper's quick bullet. An August sun, a tender breeze, the quiver of a white moth. Time to go.

5. THE WEIGHT

Abandoned by leaves and fruit and flowers
trees stretch their arms out to meet me.
It's winter. Birds, like promiscuous lovers
flit from elm to oak. I push through the waist
high snow, drop my pillow at the linden's base.
Easing my back into its welcoming trunk
I close my eyes waiting for spring.

6. PORT HOOD

At the beach nature's bell calls. Shale sheds layers of years and tears of unknown lives. At the graveyard c. 1800 a moss covered inscription pleads: *Pray for Us*. Prayers for the dead, I ask, in this mournful place where I see more dead than living.

7. A NATIONAL PASTIME

They're rioting in Vancouver. Smashing glass,
burning cars, bloodying each other.
Not like the Syrians, Egyptians or Yemenies
storming the streets. No, these ones are
pissed over a hockey game. Not food, not life,
not even damn democracy. Just Mac makeup
and designer bags.

8. HOW WILL I KNOW

One day I will not feel the warm sun on my face
the touch of a finger on my knee, the blink of my eyes,
the in and out of my breath. I will not see the squirrel scurry
tightrope-style along the high wire or hear the chickadee's sweet call,
or feel the cool breeze flowing across my naked body
lying in a muddle of leaves.

9. LADY ON THE NUMBER 3

Faded green trench coat.
Worn, wrinkled black hands,
wedding band no longer fits.
She talks quietly, so softly to herself
on the bus in the rain. Her black leather purse
old and wearing thin. Its side pockets bulging:
in one, wild cherrydrops, the other, old letters—
bundles of old letters.

10. CAROLYN

She keeps her teeth in her pocketbook.
She didn't need them, except on mornings
like this when she was having her photo taken.
It was 8-dot-dot-15.
That's how she reads digital clocks.
She lingers around the doorway,
pushes her trolley along the hall,
past the exit sign, the ice machine,
the elevator and the crib sitting for five days now.
But there was progress: it was folded and hidden in a corner.
Saved from the shake and rattle of another unwilling baby.

11. LINCOLN, MAINE

Named for Abraham,
the man they say freed the slaves.
Mill workers here have lots of money.
They buy adornments for their
homes and their RVs.
Niggerlips for their trucks:
the thing to have in this town
named for the man who freed the slaves.

12. GARDEN PICNIC AT MEADOWBANK, PEI

White swans and yellow ducks.
Black ceramic people
on white and blue
ceramic benches.
They sit properly in twos
(neatly mowed grass underfoot)
among assorted animals—
all silent, as if waiting for a cue to begin.

13. POSTCARD HOME

Mrs. Smith lived next door to Mrs. Wilson.
Mrs. Wilson told Mrs. Smith about her son.
He went to Canada. Montreal.

Found himself a little girlfriend
who knew her way around.
Wrote me a postcard, then phoned
an' said *Mamma please don't tell my wife.*

14. EASTER SUNDAY MORNING

Realizing you can
swim upstream
just as the stream
begins to dry up.

15. FOR SALE

The Baptist Church
in Rockport, Maine.
Sign says something about
The Lord and the Light.
Maybe the folks
thought the Light went out
or were the rates of faith
just too high.

FACING MY OWN POVERTY

In Matanzas Cuba,
small houses set upon
narrow sidewalks
doors open wide, or a crack.
Many faces in each room
some sad, others stare out
with curious eyes.
Black faces too
I face my past.
My 135mm camera stops
on its way to my eye.
I fear what will be
reflected in the lens.
Small, Black and dusty girl
short dress, ashen legs
long braided black hair,
looking down a rocky hill
at the car below.
White faces peer upwards,
cameras wedged between us.
They don't come out of the car.
Taking pictures of poverty.

Now, I look from a distance
through my long lens.
They may not see me.
Now, Black looks at Black
and finds no comfort.
Later, I see clothes
strung out on a rope line,
a slender, branchless tree,
a prop, to hold up the line.

And Where Am I?

I was fourteen when Malcolm X was murdered. I didn't know him then. Later in that b/w film when he asked me *where did you get your name*, I had no answer. Tarbaby, Sambo, Aunt Jemima, Uncle Ben, Topsy—they weren't my name but that's what people called me. *Don't let anyone call you out of your name,* the Sunday School mothers said. *You got but two cheeks, defend yourself.* When I told my white grade four teacher that, she didn't believe me, strapped me anyway.

A cross is burning on the lawn
next door. A little black man with
a red-chipped bowler hat and a fishing pole
sits on the veranda watching,
the paint melting from his face:
the heat, if only it were winter again.

POTATO LADY

dusty brown potato
white eyes protruding
she turns it in
her hand, knife poised
and thinks of Mary Postell
sold for a bushel of potatoes.

1.

I didn't know what a library card was. We had no library, had not been to one. The only books we had were school books, and the odd *Bobbsey Twins*. And *Bambi*, a prize for best marks in Grade 3. The *Bible* of course: a little red leather-covered pocket-sized, *New Testament,* a gift given when baptized. Inside you could write your name and date.

2.

At the front of the class, above the blackboard in the two-room school, hung a large pastel-coloured wall map of Canada. On the windowless wall, a landscape-style painting of muted sky and ghostly trees. Maybe a reproduction of one of the Group of Seven. On the opposite wall a bank of windows. A long hooked pole opened the one at the top. Who got to wield that pole, or to clean the blackboard became the stuff of schoolyard buzz: *Teacher's pet, you bet.*

3.

Harlequin romances, James Bond's adventures, comics—*Henry, Little Lulu, The Hulk, Fantastic Four.* Rarely *Superman* and *Superwoman. Mad* magazine with Spy vs Spy. James Baldwin, Gore Vidal, Ernskine Caldwell, Jacqueline Susann. Is that why it's so hard to get rid of my books, or to mark in them when reading. As if they belonged to someone else.

I don't hear the soft train whistle anymore. The squish
of brakes on the trolley car, the thud and clack of ice chunks
as the Iceman cometh. The call-in swap shop voices on the radio,
buy and sell just about anything. The tiny porcelain figurines
hidden in boxes of Red Rose tea. The ornate miniature bottles of
perfume from the Avon lady. The quiet scrape of the pencil
sharpener, a perfect curl of shaving floating to the floor. The
savour and sizzle of crisp pork scraps, fried with sweet onions
and smoked fillets on Good Friday morning. The snap of sheets
folded from the clothesline, just before the sprinkle of a summer
rain. Red hula hoops, skipping ropes and spring slush. Jawbreakers,
Lucky Bites and Tom Thumb chips from the corner store.
Midnight watch service and a single gunshot to welcome the new year.

I was bored. I found a recipe I wrote on the back of the poetry packet from the workshop. Sounds good. Quinoa Salad with Chicken: $1/4$ cup olive oil, minced garlic—one clove or

more, to taste, $1/2$ tsp paprika, $1/2$ tsp cayenne, 1 red pepper finely diced, 1 cup black beans, well rinsed and drained, a generous squeeze of lime juice, 1 cup red quinoa—

cooked and cooled, $1/2$ cup diced cooked chicken and $1/4$ cup chopped coriander. In between talk of the short lyric, old love poems, emotional truths, repetition, the rhetorical,

and Sappho, who someone said started this whole mess, was the last instruction: *Who's brave enough to try a ghazal?* Think I'll try the recipe.

For Shani

You won't find heirloom silver, Royal Albert China or a cut-glass crystal vase—all trashed in exchange for that second-hand leather-bound copy of *Nicholas Nickleby* in its original ornate well-kept box. *A History of Art Impressionism*, essential to answer her question: *How do I define 'neo-impressionism'*. A fat, ragged, coverless dictionary, the first page of the 'u' is missing. Spelling bee lists and dictée for Grade 5. The last dregs of morning coffee asleep in the handleless chipped pottery cup, I should toss but can't. There's the Crayola box, but Blizzard Blue, Burnt Sienna and Desert Sand are missing. The remains of the last Halloween costume when you dressed up as Quasimodo's sister: glue gun, glitter, silky blue ribbons. A reminder letter about winter soccer. In a hundred years what will the archeologist decide went on here?

SOLONGONE

Been away from home longer than my memory

       my mother's memory

             my grandmother's memory.

       So long gone. Still I remember—

Awakened by the pulsing tam tam, surging like an electric current
                          across centuries.

       I am who they imagined.

Some of these poems have appeared in the following journals and anthologies: *The Dalhousie Review, Daughters of the Sun, Women of the Moon, Fire on the Water, Fiery Spirits, Fireweed, Other Voices, The Great Black North, Temba Tupu, To Find Us* and *West Coast Line*. Grateful thanks to the editors involved. Several poems from this collection were part of *Excavation: A Site of Memory*, my multi-media installation at the Dalhousie Art Gallery in October 2013. ¶ Special thanks to Dionne Brand and George Elliott Clarke who generously read an early version of this manuscript. Thanks to Jan Zwicky and Tim Lilburn who commented on some of these poems during workshops in Kentville, Nova Scotia, and Banff, Alberta. ¶ Thanks to Anne Simpson for her encouragement. ¶ Enormous thanks and gratitude to everyone at Gaspereau Press for their care and attention, and for believing in this work. ¶ To my family, Bev, Shani, Ada, Janet, Wayne and Wayn, Rugi, Alf, Marie Nita Waldron, Gerald Mac Hamilton, and the ever-growing Hamilton contingent, you have my heart now and always. And to my ancestors, I am, only because you were. Thank you.

The title, AND I ALONE ESCAPED TO TELL YOU is taken from a verse in the Book of Job, 1:15 (RSV, 1962).

The epigraph VOYAGE THROUGH DEATH TO LIFE UPON THESE SHORES is taken from Robert Hayden's epic poem "Middle Passage," first published in *Phylon* in 1945.

The phrase SLAVES BY HABIT AND EDUCATION is taken from a letter sent by Lord Dalhousie to the Earl of Bathurst about the Black Refugees from the War of 1812. Lord Dalhousie was Nova Scotia's lieutenant governor from 1816–20.

An advertisement for a 'slave auction' where young Black girls were being sold at Halifax's waterfront was published in a Halifax paper and is referenced in T.W. Smith's *The Slave In Canada*.

The epigraph that begins section three is from a speech delivered in 1954 by Pablo Neruda at the dedication ceremonies for the Pablo Neruda Foundation for the Study of Poetry at the University of Chile in Santiago.

Mary Postell was a free Black Loyalist in Nova Scotia who went to court twice to fight for her freedom in 1785–86; she lost both times and was eventually re-enslaved and sold by Samuel Gray to William Mangrum for one hundred pounds of potatoes, valued at twenty pounds.

Some of these poems were informed by historical sources, including T.W. Smith's "The Slave in Canada" in *Collections of the Nova Scotia Historical Society* 10 (1899); C.B. Ferguson's *A Documentary Study of the Establishment of the Negroes in Nova Scotia between the War of 1812 and the Winning of Responsible Government* (Halifax: Public Archives of Nova Scotia, publication no. 8, 1948); and C.B. Ferguson's (editor) *Clarkson's Mission to America, 1791–1792* (Halifax: Public Archives of Nova Scotia, publication no. 11, 1971). Archival records related to the Black Loyalists and the Black Refugees of the War of 1812 (also known as the Chesapeake Blacks) are found at the Public Archives of Nova Scotia. Some are now available online at http://www.novascotia.ca/nsarm/virtual/africanns/

SDH

7 6 5 4 3 2

Library and Archives Canada Cataloguing in Publication

Hamilton, Sylvia, 1950–, author
    And I alone escaped to tell you / Sylvia Hamilton.

Poems.
ISBN 978-1-55447-136-2 (pbk.)

    1. Black Canadians—Nova Scotia—Poetry. I. Title.

PS8615.A4428A5 2014   C811'.6   C2014-901865-7

GASPEREAU PRESS LIMITED ¶ GARY DUNFIELD
& ANDREW STEEVES ¶ PRINTERS & PUBLISHERS
47 CHURCH AVENUE KENTVILLE NS B4N 2M7
Literary Outfitters & Cultural Wilderness Guides

Date Due

BRODART, CO. Cat. No. 23-233 Printed in U.S.A.